10 LIFE HACKS TO

BEAT THE MATRIX

TEN SIMPLE LIFE
HACKS
IN
WHICH TO EMPOWER
YOURSELF AND
IMPROVE YOUR LIFE

TONY SAYERS

www.transcendingtimes.org

ABOUT THE AUTHOR

Tony Sayers is a passionate activist, vlogger, writer, and public speaker who in 2013 started to become aware of the deeper goings-on within this World and the hidden hands that control it. Since having these realisations he has been relentless in his work to expose the levels of corruption in society in an attempt to help others open their eyes. He is driven by doing what he can in his own way to help future generations enjoy a better World. His work has been mainly focused on human psychology, mind control, and spiritual laws. He is now progressing into technological, metaphysical manipulations, and energy healing work.

Born in Southend on Sea, Essex, UK he enjoyed a good childhood, although he found school quite challenging with other students and somewhat boring. His questioning of what is 'normal' had subconsciously already begun. From school, Tony went traveling when he was 21 which was a huge learning curve where he felt he got a real education observing how other cultures lived, and the vast differences between the developed and non-developed World. He also traveled to Nepal and researched Buddhism, which at the time which was to sew a spiritual seed in him that was to germinate later in life. After this period he went on to work in many standard jobs in both the Banking and Estate Agency Worlds, but never truly felt fulfilled, and feeling as if he was just going through the motions of life. It was in this period where he was so downbeat in the rigorous daily grind he started to ask the big questions in life which ultimately led him to these greater understandings about himself and the World, the learning is still going on today.

Sometimes controversial Tony is raw in how he expresses himself and his truth but is always coming from a place of care and desire for positive change. Tony has appeared on radio shows and spoke publicly which can be found on YouTube. He has his own website which is http://www.transcendingtimes.org where all his work can be found. To Subscribe To subscribe to his free weekly newsletter which has blogs, vlogs, media announcements and information on up and coming books just join here https://transcendingtimes.org/subscribe-to- newsletters/

Tony recently authored his first book 'Are You Living Or Just Existing?' which is available in paperbook, kindle, and ebook format and can be found here https://transcendingtimes.org/books/

Introduction

So having spent the last 6 years exposing copious amounts of corruption, lies, and propaganda across many different areas I often get asked the question 'well what can we do'? With so much hysteria and turmoil seemingly around us, how can we protect and empower ourselves? This ebook details really what I have found on my own journey, some of these techniques may or may not work for you, many of them are simply just common sense, but if we have the willpower and desire to evolve then we can level up in what is essentially this simulated computer game we find ourselves in.

That really is the way we need to look at things here in this holographic reality, we are all players in the game and we all have a simple choice either to keep doing what we have always done and stay on level one, or put in the hard work which also potentially means sacrifice to level up.

See what I found on my own journey is that you cannot have one without the other. What I mean by this is that we can only go some way in changing the World unless we also change ourselves. Much of the Worlds turmoil and suffering is undoubtedly being manipulated by a cabal and mindless henchmen humans that have lost the ability to discern right from wrong that is without question. But I also feel so much suffering is also simply a manifestation of what is going on inside of us, traumas and emotions we carry into adult life from childhood. We project this out onto the World through anger, insecurities, and addictions adding to the toxicity of the collective. If we want peace without we also need to have peace within.

This is powerful...

So much of this ebook is about how we can both shield and empower ourselves to combat the current insanity of the World, how we can grow, heal, and ultimately get to a place where we can stand firm and resolute in our core, reconnect with the essence within, and rediscover our humanity once again.

Because this is both a big part of the problem and the solution in that we have forgotten who we really are.

We are the artists, the painters, the writers, the comedians, the poets, and the storytellers. We are not just 9-5 rats stuck in a race working in jobs we hate with people we don't like. We are, at our essence, genius that has forgotten that it is genius. Wonderful creative, loving, and strong beings who have been hoodwinked into thinking that they are insignificant. This has to end, and perhaps the biggest part to escaping the Matrix for good is if we all reconnect with who we REALLY are again. But in order to do this, we have to go through a process of undoing, we have to disconnect from the lies and then heal on multiple levels. Of course, we need to continue shining the light on the dark that is a given, but we must work on ourselves too.

As we light up ourselves, we allow and hold space for others to do the same. These are incredibly exciting and fascinating times to be alive, we are seeing hundreds if not thousands of years of darkness coming to the surface. I feel that although it appears to be getting worse on the surface, it is actually in its death throws. This should not be a time to fear, its a time for opportunity and growth, the Matrix is not as all-powerful as it appears, and if you're smart and have willpower along with perseverance, then many aspects of it can be transcended.

Hopefully, this ebook will give you some ideas in order to make your own life easier and help you become more solution based than stuck in the problem.

CONTENTS

PHYSICAL HEALTH

This one really is a no-brainer, if we are to be at our best and function to maximum capabilities then it is imperative that we look after our physical health. Our bodies literally are our temples which house our consciousness for this lifetime, and if you want to be happier, connect with your higher-self easier, and have more energy to get things done then it is a must for everyone. Being physically in good shape gives us that extra drive to find our purpose, in turn we can then execute what we have to do. How can we expect to deal with what this reality brings if we are constantly sick?

This is something that has surprised me within the alternative media in that how many people realise that there are poisonous chemicals in food products, alcohol, and cigarettes yet continue to consume. Not only are they destroying themselves but are also giving their power and energy away to these evil corporations that sell us these toxins.

Let me say now I'm not 100% perfect and I doubt anybody is, we all have our treats every now and then, but it becomes a problem when the treats are our daily norm. I understand that if you have a craving then it is hard to break, but that craving is coming from a part of you that is unhappy which then means there is emotional/inner child work that needs to be done.

For me, a plant-based diet changed my life, rewind back 5 years ago and I was a different person, I was eating meat, crisps, sweets etc Give me a vegetable and I would have thrown it out of the window! The offshoot was I was becoming sick, digestive issues and acid reflux tormented me. My blood pressure was high and I knew things had to change.

Luckily enough for me, I had already started to become aware of how the pharmaceutical industry was in bed with the food industry. How through the so- called 'food' we are eating it is making people sick. Heart disease, cancer, and diabetes are all on the rise from just 20 years ago, there has to be a reason for this and that is because most of our food is fake, its just masquerading as food!

Full of artificial sweeteners, excitotoxins, and GMOS. What we are consuming is Frankenstein food at best! The cat is long out of the bag now in terms of the food deception and if we are serious about changing both ourselves and the Planet then we need to reject these toxins as much as possible.

I write extensively about the damage alcohol is doing to us not only as individuals but society as a whole in my book 'Are You Living Or Just Existing? That   is without the spiritual connotations of being out of your centre which opens you up to distorted energies (they don't call them spirits for nothing!) It destroys your liver which is essential for cleaning your body and also helps with metabolism amongst other things. Alcohol is advertised everywhere even at events that are supposed to promote health, yet it is such a destructive disease in society, it has its

tentacles in literally every aspect of our lives. Weddings, funerals, weekends, relaxing, meals out, and even meals in all seem to revolve around getting drunk! Again this also needs to be rejected if you're serious about becoming the best version of yourself and if we as a society want to evolve to anything greater than what we currently are.

For my own health all my physical ailments cleared up when I gave up meat, the acid reflux went away immediately (meat is acidic by its very nature, and an acidic environment in the body is the main cause of cancer) I had more energy throughout the day instead of feeling tired and lethargic, and I distinctly remember a noticeable shift in the quality of my thoughts. I felt I was downloading much clearer from my higher self, and that my thoughts became more positive. The benefits have continued until today where I can honestly say I feel healthier now than I did 10 years ago.

Of course, there are a number of ethical reasons why we should give up eating flesh. Factory farming and overfishing is destroying the Planet faster than anything else as we panic to try to provide for the growing population. Acres of woodland and rainforest are being cleared by the second for cattle farming, and it is estimated that by 2040 most of the fish in the oceans will be gone. This is the reality we face, so a massive instant solutionary change a person could make for themselves, future generations, and the World's environment is to transition to a plant-based diet.

Of course, its important to be discerning in plant-based choices also, the movement has grown exponentially year on year and the greedy corporations along with the food industry who like us to be sick have realised this. There is now a massive plethora of plant-based alternatives available now, and much of this is junk just replacing one toxin with another. There is a big push on fake meat also which I don't trust as far as I can throw! The closer to Nature the better in my view, even that's not easy with pesticides and herbicides in the west, and organic can also be far from that these days also. We just need to research, take our time, and discern these things thoroughly. But changing your diet will elevate you to health you may not have known before, it did with me and the only regret I have is that I didn't do it sooner.

Let food be thy medicine & medicine be thy food
Hippocerates

Now a good diet without regular exercise goes without saying, getting the body moving detoxes the body, and in my view detoxes the mind. It gets the endorphins flowing and an all round feel good factor pumping. I have always found that any problems or stress in my life is dramatically eased after exercise. The key from my experience to maintaining a regular routine is to do something you enjoy, even if its just walking. For me, I love to swim, hike, and play football and its less of a wrench on my day if I do these activities. On the other hand, try getting me down the gym regularly or jogging and I can't stand it!

Reducing stress levels is another aspect of health that is not spoken about too often, our cells react to and absorb our emotions, and let's face it most of society is stuck in 'fight or flight' mode which then has a huge impact on the adrenals and nervous system. We need to be very wary of this, if you eat well and exercise but your stress levels are through the roof then you have only solved part of the puzzle. For me, a walk in Nature is the perfect remedy for this along with some kind of spiritual practice such as meditation or yoga.

Then we also have the issue of the water we drink, let's face it most of us just turn on the tap water and automatically expect it to be safe to drink, I mean its been through the 'treatment' process after all. You trust that because you pay your water rates you are therefore going to get your money's worth in pure clean water.

A few years ago my own research led me to the conclusion that in actual fact tap water is pretty toxic. Picking up dirt from old pipes en route to your home, and even more concerning containing a cocktail of neurotoxins which have been sold to us as something beneficial for our health, for example, fluoride and chlorine. Fluoride, in particular, has been marketed in a way that is an absolute necessity for strong clean teeth, hmm I wonder if that's the reason why there is a poison warning on the back of toothpaste packaging with warning signs for children that if they swallow any then they should go to the doctors or hospital?! Doesn't sound very beneficial to me!

The truth is fluoride is a devastating neurotoxin that can pretty much disintegrate concrete in enough volumes, yet there it is in our tap water. The question is WHY and why have we been lied to in such a monumental way? This isn't just me saying this a quick search on Google or YouTube will bring up reams of information about this. It really is sad that we have to become detectives when checking the quality of our basic needs in life these days, we just assume that the government has our best interests at heart and will provide the very best for us. Unfortunately its quite clear now that the opposite is true, and it is down to us all individually to really take responsibility in what we are putting in our bodies and those of our family members.

Here you can see an experiment which will show you exactly what is in your tap water (at least if you live in the UK) I used a water distiller (which for me are by far the best way to produce good clean water) if you're interested in finding out more about them here is the company I recommend

https://www.makewaterpure.co.uk/?ref=dENUOW42MER MZG89

There is so much I could talk about when it comes to physical wellbeing but I am just attempting to outlay the fundamental basics that require our attention. The final aspect of importance on this topic for me is detoxing. This is something that has helped me really motor forward with my health.

There are literally hundred of detoxes out there, I could write another book on them all, you have to research and choose one that is right for you. I would suggest a short one if it is your first time, maybe just even for 24 hours and then work your way up from there. Many people make the mistake of diving head first into a 2-week water fast and then get sick.

The issue here is that most peoples bodies are so full of toxins that if you dramatically come off food like that then you will be sick, the reason is that we never give the body a chance to dispell toxins with our 3 meal a day diet in the west. It is constantly in digestion mode therefore always working on that. When we stop and give it a break it cannot wait to rid the toxic overload and the body gets overwhelmed.

The correct way to do it is to slowly come off food on the days leading up to the detox with light salads and then maybe juices. Also do the same when you start eating again, slowly come onto solids as to not overwhelm the body.

The physical health arena is huge and everyone has their own views and opinions, these techniques I researched myself and have been solid in my own personal growth, but I encourage to do your own research, and ultimately make the decision to become healthier as it will then permeate positively in all other aspects of your life.

"Health is not valued until sickness comes."

-Thomas Fuller

EMOTIONAL/INNER CHILD WORK

Why is it so important to heal your inner child? What can healing the inner child bring to our lives? I have been on a huge journey over the past 2 years, it has been the most transformational of my life. Down the paths of both self-healing and energy work has really helped me see the bigger picture in this whole Matrix game, and that it is often times the biggest battles are with ourselves and more importantly, any long-term changes and any healing of the World will only come when we heal ourselves as I have said previously.

The Universal Law of correspondence dictates 'as above, so below' Is it any wonder the World is in so much pain and suffering when many of us are as individuals? To raise our vibration and to get in touch with our core essence means essentially we move beyond the game. Of course, there are many manipulations that need to be worked through on both the surface level and in the etheric, and I am not for one second propagating the whole 'New Age' idea of ignoring everything that is negative and just focusing on ourselves. No, this inner work needs to be done in TANDEM with helping others.

To heal your inner child is to me the ultimate expression of self-love, and to put it bluntly without which we are never going to become a truly whole and balanced person, constantly having our parts triggered by others lashing out from unhealed wounds, even if this on a subconscious level.

Healing that little boy or girl that has been crying out for your attention for years is so pivotal to your own future happiness. We are ALL wounded to different degrees, I used to think I was ok, yeah I had a few things happen to me but nothing major (I thought) compared to others. That's life right? WRONG you will attract people, circumstances, situations into your life based around your unhealed parts. You will go through life being triggered by your unhealed parts, and you will look to others to try and heal those unhealed parts which of course no partner, family member, or spouse could ever do, and ultimately it is unfair to expect them to. Surely its time to sort our baggage out that has been holding us back all our lives? We deserve to be happy, fulfilled, and have the very best relationships.

This work has been so powerful for me I decided I wanted to help others too, I am far less triggered and reactive, I care much less about what people think about me and feel secure in my own skin, and although the healing never really ends as such I feel secure knowing that I will attract better relationships, and can show up as my best version and that I am not projecting my childhood wounds and fears.   I   was   delighted   to complete the psychotherapy course where I am now helping to empower others and help them work past the aspects of their subconscious that are holding them back, and at the same time reconnect with more of their true essence. Feel free to contact me for more information about this if you're interested.

Emotional work or lack thereof it is particularly prominent in men. Men will avoid emotional work like the plague! It really is the elephant in the room, I mean who wants to look at their shadows right?!

But why do men avoid emotional work so much? It is said that women are twice as likely to work on their emotional shadows than men. The whole macho image is all well and good until you take a step back and realise that actually as men, persisting with this social stigma is not only damaging to ourselves in our search relationships, people in our life, and who we draw in on unhealed wounds.

Imagine the kind of relationships we could have if we weren't projecting all that pent-up sadness and anger we have been told to suppress as men. Imagine we actually owned and dealt with our stuff so we could feel happiness at a deep level and not just on a superficial level, papering over the cracks with drugs, alcohol, food, or whatever the vice might be? Because that's what we as men do, we turn to these plasters as solutions. We as men will try and stuff, bury, and avoid our demons. Men want to fix things rather than talking them through or attempt to deal with them. I'm sure many women reading this will agree with me!

Just as important as the physical body is the emotional state, gyms all around the World are packed with people who are very concerned about how they look physically when perhaps it could be argued that many of them are emotionally dead inside. The truth is we can only deeply love another to the direct amount we have deeply gone into ourselves and most people sadly have not even scratched the surface. This is just simply because of how society is set up. We live in the age of the 'selfie' the age of the filtered Instagram photo, everything is about our outside shells and that cannot be right. We create and manifest from the inwards out not the other way around, and this is fundamentally what is wrong with most people on this Planet who don't realize this. Until we inner stand that truth and do what we need to do to face the dark night of our souls and heal then we are always swimming against the tide both individually and collectively. Heal your emotional subconscious self and get more of what you say you want in life, otherwise you're leaving it to chance at best.

The conflict we encounter in our relationships with others is an invitation to acknowledge and heal the hurt child within, with love, care and courage.

transcendingtimes.org

PROTECT YOUR ENERGY

I n these increasingly hostile times protecting your energy and vibration should be paramount. But what are we protecting our energy from exactly and why?

Now, this isn't scaremongering this is just realising that we are involved in all-out spiritual warfare.

It's important to inner stand that human energy, particularly lower vibration emotions like fear, anger, and stress are basically FOOD for entities, attachments, and parasitic forces just outside of our visible sight. There is a very good reason that this Planet exists in the constant state of fear as it does, and that is because these parasitic energies need it to exist.

I won't be the first person to speak of these issues, and I certainly won't be the last, these entities have had many names throughout history and many references most notably demons, flyers, and jinn. These have the ability to heavily influence a persons behavior, belief systems, or ultimately if the person has been traumatized enough, or has allowed themselves to become so 'off centre' maybe through alcohol or drug abuse, can either partially or fully take over a person.

If you don't believe me then just type into Youtube 'Flacca drug'. Here you basically see what a full demonic takeover is essentially where the person even seems to develop superhuman strengths! To protect your energy efficiently really does mean questioning everything that we have just accepted as normal human behavior.

Now, of course, that is an extreme example but you can scale that down to alcohol, look at the word 'spirits' and drinking 'gin' as I mentioned previously. The same spirits that can parasite from you when you're off your center drunk? Or could it be the Jinn in your GIN and tonic? Absolutely I would say, indeed the word 'alcohol' is said to come from the Arabic term 'Al Khul' which means body eating spirit!

I'm not just talking about alcohol that opens you up to these outside forces, this won't be popular but I'm talking about things like factory made DMT, fashionable plant medicines that aren't being performed by proper Shamans and without the right integrity and intentions like Ayahuasca, I'm talking heavy weed smoking, which, like it or not, does lower your vibration (something which I had to really come to terms with myself) I'm not doubting the medicinal benefits here by the way which are not in doubt, I'm talking about smoking it all the time. Pharmaceutical drugs do a great job of lowering our vibrations, these can all open you up.

Sleeping around, watching porn is all low vibrational, where you can become corded with the other person to the point where you get to share each other's entities and karma! Why do you think this highly promiscuous sexual society is propagated everywhere? I know it's not what people want to hear but it needs to be said. We all want to feel like we can do whatever we want, and we can no doubt, we still have an element of free will. What I am saying is be aware and protect your energy. I am talking from EXPERIENCE of having worked on people who have come to me, I have seen these things in people's eyes, and their behavior. The attachments severity can be varying, some just hold us back in life constantly looping fear and anxiety back into us via the chakras which are false white light.

Some are more severe and can even make us feel suicidal.
Now things can really take a twist when you are someone on the path of truth and justice and try to make a difference in the World. As I said earlier we are in all-out SPIRITUAL

WARFARE. If you believe that this is all just playing out in the 3rd- dimensional physical reality then you only really have half the picture, as above so below, what is happening here is already going on in 4D. What I am saying is that these entities are upping their game. They know people are waking up and the last thing they want is for us to move towards the condition of love and harmony. Why? NO FOOD. It's too high a vibration for them, so you can bet your bottom dollar they will be throwing a spanner in the works of anyone who is trying to nudge humanity along towards that very condition. What am I talking about here? Well, ladies and gentlemen allow me to introduce you to the World of the "Alien Love Bite"!

In a nutshell what I am talking about here is where someone comes into your life and appears, on the surface at least, to be everything you ever wanted. There is a resonance and a feeling like you have met 'the one' then as time goes by you start to see subtle changes in that person, and not good ones at that, until a few months in you are now dealing with a complete narcissist, sociopath, or even psychopath who throws your life into utter upset and turmoil! Completely taking you off your path, or trying to at least where you become so disillusioned it can take months or even years to fully recover!

This isn't just a normal breakup, I mean if you try and break up with a love bite be prepared for smear campaigns, your name to be trashed, or just a complete annihilation of your character and work. Why? Because that was their very role to begin with. They were so toxic inside that these parasitic forces were pulling their strings. They never wanted YOU as such, they wanted YOU off your path.

So have fun by all means but always consider your energy. Is this person good for my energy? Is this food? Is this sexual partner? Are these drugs? These days I try to keep in my center as much as possible, I don't drink, do drugs, to be fair I did all that in my 20s and its overrated anyway! All I'm saying is there are potential consequences with these things that we don't fully understand because we are not educated in the metaphysical. Keeping your energy clean will mean you have more of it to direct to your purpose and evolving into a better human.

ACCEPTANCE

This is certainly not to be confused with the 'New Age' pseudo spirituality toxic ideology of literally just accepting ANYTHING and that there is no good or evil or right and wrong. That is seriously dangerous thinking and one many people who get attracted to that scene fall into.

It is cowardice and total avoidance which really is at the root of the New Age movement. Just people running away from their own issues and that of the World, it gives them a free pass to stand by as the World goes up in flames just thinking happy fluffy thoughts about flying unicorns and gong baths!

This is not the type of acceptance I am talking about here, I am talking about if something is wrong then it absolutely must be changed, however, if you have gone as far as you can with something or a particular person then sometimes choosing our battles wisely is the only option.

At the crux of this issue is what many of us in the alternative media face and that is attempting to get others to see what we can see. (I don't like the phrase to wake someone up, the etymology of the word 'wake' means something you have after someone's death which indicates to me that this is a SPELL-ing which probably does the opposite of what we want it to do when we say it!)

I can talk first hand about this having fallen out in some way or another with most people in my life through desperately trying to get them to see the light. In hindsight, it has damaged me. It caused me no end of stress and frustration constantly banging the 'truth drum' only for it to fall on deaf ears. It made me a very angry person which only fed back into the Matrix and unseen forces.

There is that old cliché saying 'you can lead a horse to water but you cannot make it drink' this is so true and I really wish I had listened to people when they said it to me. I don't think I will ever stop speaking my truth and I will never be able to fully censor myself, but I've found the best coping mechanism is just to walk away in the end.

If people cannot see the insanity right in front of their faces now then quite frankly they are ignoring it, and it matters not how much information you stick in front of their noses. You cannot make somebody care, they have to have that within themselves, some people will walk through the door you open and others won't.

Those that don't will have to face the consequences whatever they maybe. It is their karma and you have done your job by showing them the door in the first place. Focus on new people to reach and just distance yourself.

The way I see things is that you're either on the field of play or you're not, and continuing to present golden eggs to blind ignorance and avoidance is only damaging you. Anyone not willing to enter the field of play is siding with the enemy, its that cut and dry for me now. There doesn't have to be a big fuss or argument its just a mismatch is resonance.

Sometimes things are actually just out of our control and its learning to recognize if something can be changed or not, which then goes back to the previous point of protecting your energy. Continuing on with something that deep down you know is a waste of time is draining your energy. This applies to relationships and family too and nothing is more important than protecting your energy.

GRANT ME
THE SERENITY
TO ACCEPT THE THINGS
I CANNOT CHANGE,
THE COURAGE TO CHANGE
THE THINGS I CAN, AND
THE WISDOM TO KNOW
THE DIFFERENCE.

-NIEBUHR-

RAISE YOUR VIBRATION

When you realise that this whole reality is designed to keep us in a low vibration its good practice to try where possible not to buy into it all. Again we are living in a realm where there is a lot going on than just the physical. Unseen parasites lurk in 4D harvesting on all the low vibrational energy we omit be it fear, anger, or even low vibrational sexual energy through porn.

Again this isn't to say that we have to ignore the suffering of others not at all, it just means that we are almost in this World but not of it. We see the suffering and craziness going on around us but we don't feed the energy vampires. Its not easy and very much like walking a tightrope. So often on my journey, especially in the early days, I have gone down a rabbit hole and let it affect me. This really only feeds one thing and that is the Matrix and its forces.

When we vibrate at a higher frequency we move out of their feeding zones, we go beyond the Matrix in a sense. This is why there is such a battle on this Planet right now, people are raising their consciousness which then helps to raise their frequency, and if we can do this on a mass scale well then, its game over for the parasites!

There are many ways to raise your vibration as you can see in the above picture which provides a number of ideas on what works and what doesn't. I feel there are more permanent aspects of life we also need to look at to hold a higher vibration too.

These would be things like am I happy where I am living? This is a big one for me, I literally cannot function in certain Countries, I am very energy sensitive so if I get stuck somewhere out of alignment my mood will drop. That why I choose to live in South East Asia because the energy, people, and weather all suit me and I can thrive. For other people it maybe different but my point is that if you're not happy in your immediate environment then it will always be more difficult to raise your vibration.

I fully appreciate it's not always easy to just get up and leave. We have commitments, children maybe, and financially things might be a bit tight. But it is something worth thinking about, and if you're not happy where you are and it's viable to move then you should do it! Plus a change of scenery I feel is always good for the soul journey.

Another little hack that worked for me was when I sold all my stuff. So many of us own way more than we need, mainly due to society telling us that we need to consume all the time. So our homes become cluttered with junk, and then if we do ever want to move we have to think about ferrying all the junk around with us!

I live a minimalistic lifestyle nowadays meaning you can pretty much pack all my belongings in one big rucksack! It wasn't always like that, I had the Mercedes car, loads of clothes and shoes, and generally loads of junk I just did not need that I had accumulated over the years. Over time I sold or got rid of it all, and let me tell you it is liberating!

If I want to move around I am not bound by 'stuff' and also the financial debt that all that stuff brings too. Also, there is something positive energetically with having a home which is free from junk, the Japanese recognise it just look into Feng Shui.

Again I am going to mention this as it has been key to me raising my own vibration and that is emotional/inner child work again. How can you honestly expect to keep a higher frequency if you're constantly being triggered or attracting negative people/experiences into your life based around unhealed emotions and traumas? I understand its probably the last thing people want to hear but I can speak from first-hand experience that this is key to being able to maintain a higher vibration because your all round life experiences improve.

Animals are always good for me too. I have 5 dogs here Thailand and just being around them raises me up a notch or two, especially when we all go for a walk out in Nature then you get the best of both Worlds. Whatever you love to do make sure you make time for it in your busy life, for example just a ten-minute meditation can set up your day in a really good way. We often get so caught up in our lives we forget to make time for the things that actually make us feel good. Don't let this be you, starve those parasites and set aside some time in your day specifically to raise your vibration then commit to it, you deserve it!

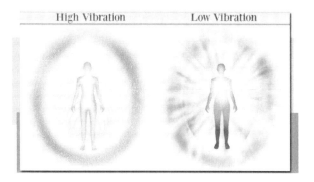

BUILD YOUR SPIRITUAL CORE

Building your spiritual core strengthens your connection to essence which is essentially who you really are, it takes us into a deeper part of ourselves that is the TRUE self. It reminds us that no matter how insane things are here at times we are much more than just a human body. Its a well of unconditional love, strength, and understanding that is infinite. It enables us to cope far better in this reality and helps us see that when all is said and done this really is just a game we are playing, albeit on one level a very real one.

It enables us to live in the moment and connect with the simplicity of just being rather than doing. We can take a step back from the monkey mind and just observe, we can see that most of the time our thoughts are not even our own and are our parts, triggers, unhealed wounds, or deepest subconscious fears. We can evaluate from this point what we need to do in order to transcend these thoughts.

Strengthening your core also builds a stronger defense against parasitic entities and interdimensional interference as you both raise your frequency, and move out of negative emotions towards calmness and peacefulness.

It can produce great insights and downloads as you're much more able to connect with your higher self and any higher frequency energies that want to interact with you. I would say finding a spiritual practice that helps to strengthen your core isn't just something you need to do every now and then, it should be part of your weekly schedule.

There are many modalities and like exercise, it is down to you to find one that you enjoy and one that works for you. I recently attended a 7-day meditation retreat which did wonders for me. I really learned the art of patience as you cannot even speak to anyone for the whole time, and there is literally nothing else going on other than meditation. Something like that can catapult your spiritual progress and strengthen that core. I now try to incorporate it into my daily life.

Ten Life Hacks To Beat The Matrix

Martial arts are also good for this, particularly something like tai-chi. Many of these combats use core strength and a spiritual discipline which in my view make them all the more powerful.

See looking after yourself mentally, emotionally, physically, and spiritually is really what is at the core of this book. Its a bit like spinning plates in a sense, we always need to keep an eye on ourselves and check in where we need to give ourselves more attention. The more empowered we become on all levels the easier it is to combat and then transcend stuff that holds us back. As we progress we become a shining light that others can then follow. We raise our vibration, step into our power, and are much more able to be of help to others and the Planet as a whole.

DISCONNECT TO RECONNECT

Unfortunately, we live in a radioactive soup these days, we are literally surrounded by technology, distorted electromagnetic fields, and wherever you go in the World you can pretty much guarantee there will be a WIFI connection nearby! The issue is that we don't really know what impact this is having on our health, research is starting to come out about the dangers of WIFI so it is a good idea if you can find time to disconnect for a while.

Research is showing that heavy exposure to cell phone radiation in rats causes tumors, hormonal changes, and oxidative stress which has been linked to brain disease and cancers. It can cause insomnia, damage cell growth, and is said to potentially cause sterilization and neutralizes sperm.

The problem is we are all addicted to the internet, I myself have to drag myself away from it after too many hours spent going down rabbit holes and scrolling down my Facebook feed, in actual fact disconnecting is something I need to do more often myself!

It has become way too convenient, and now there is a disappointment if you walk into a restaurant or cafe and there is no WIFI. I actually believe in the notion that we are actually telepathic beings, and that we were given language to replace telepathy and to cast spells (spellings) on each other. They have hoodwinked us into believing in that because of the internet, we are now more connected than ever, however, I honestly feel that as we evolve and raise in consciousness we are actually more and more in tune telepathically with each other.

How many times have you happened to think of somebody and they start calling you on your mobile phone? Or someone will pop into your head that you haven't seen in years and then you will suddenly drive past them? This is telepathy. I am convinced that telepathy is like any other skill in that the more you practice it the better we become. There have been many experiments set up that show this WIFI effects on the brain.

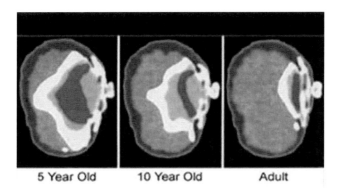

| 5 Year Old | 10 Year Old | Adult |

It is also my feeling that interdimensional interference can infiltrate our energy fields a lot easier in this radioactive soup surrounded by WIFI. It would definitely make sense that all this WIFI distorts our thinking. In the meditation retreat I recently attended there was no WIFI and I could tell the difference in the quality of my thoughts, downloads, and connection to my higher self. So for that reason alone, it is worth doing.

Just reconnecting back with Nature and the present moment, and ultimately what is real. We now live in a World where technology takes precedence over the natural World. Especially when it comes to the younger generations. Kids nowadays are more able to download an app than tell you what kind of bird they see in the back garden. This is particularly worrisome when you consider the Planet is already being trashed, so if this generation grows up not caring then it makes you wonder what will happen.

Disconnecting from technology is much more than the energetic interference also, disconnecting from social media is also great for rebooting the mind. It has become a constant distraction for many of us as we live our lives virtually more than ever. Constantly in search of more dopamine hits from likes or comments on Facebook, Instagram, or Twitter. This is especially important if you're involved with the alternative media unfortunately, these current times are often filled with raising awareness on dark matters, and if you don't break from it every now and again then you can be dragged down into an emotional downward spiral. I have been there many times before! Take time off and reconnect with you, your family, friends, pets, and the REAL World every now and then.

Take Risks

S ometimes in life you have to take a punt, I'm not for one second advocating risks that put yourself or your family in harm's way, and of course, they need to be thoroughly thought through. What I am saying is that sometimes we hold ourselves back, we get in our own way so to speak. We prevent ourselves from going after our dreams or living in line with our true purpose through fear. I love that old saying 'nothing ever grows in your comfort zone' because it is so true.

We have this false idea of safety that we have been indoctrinated with since school in that there is only one way to live life. We must get good grades, then a degree, then get married, a mortgage, 2 kids and a picket fence, and then you die. This is what is sold to us as a 'safe life' and one where we will be accepted by the rest of the herd as being 'successful'.

In reality, nothing could be further from the truth because all you're basically doing is going along with societies version of success. It's not everybody's dream to want to do these things however if it's yours then fine. What I am saying is that if everyone was truly honest with themselves then he or she might not want to

get married, have kids, or work a 9-5 corporate job because its just 'the thing to do'

We sell our souls short, our spirit feels uneasy, and we have a longing for more. Perhaps we haven't even explored our deepest desires for fear that it would possibly mean changing our whole lives around? This happens a lot, people know deep down that they're just existing but don't want to face the upheaval of change, and what others might think or say about them for wanting that.

Let's remember that the system wants people living the same kind of lives, like chickens in a free-range farm, with just an illusion of freedom. It hates people who buck the trend, walk to the beat of their own drum, and step outside the box.

I'm not just talking about drastic changes here either like turning your life upside down. It could be something small like starting to write that book you always wanted to write, painting a picture or trekking that mountain for a physical challenge. It may even be something like reconnecting with an old friend or family member that you haven't spoken to for years, or if you're single putting yourself out there more socially in order to meet somebody. My point is that we can procrastinate too much to the point we never end up doing anything.

I am a great believer, and indeed have seen proof in my own life, that if we follow our hearts desires then the Universe will offer support to us. Sometimes we just have to take the plunge and help ourselves make that first step. Life passes by extremely fast, and in my view, a life half lived is a waste. I don't have many fears, but one I do have is lying on my death bed with regrets. I don't want to be there thinking I should've written th: book, made peace with that person, or lived abroad. That scares me more than anything at all.

I can only speak from my own experience in that if I hadn't one day just given up my old life back in Essex, I wouldn't have moved to London, and I then probably wouldn't be living in Asia. I would more than likely still be there now. We have many different timelines we can shift to at any given moment, some move us more in alignment with our truth and purpose, others further away. It's about recognizing these gateway portals and walking through them without fear.

It's about developing trust that if you follow your truth then the Universe will have your back. At the very least if things don't work out then you can hold your head up high and say that you gave it your very best shot! That is the minimum anyone should ask of themselves. Tune in with your intuition and inner knowing, what is it do you really want and need right now? Is it a new job, a change of location, do you need to heal? Then take the appropriate action to set the wheels in motion.
You can do it!

STOP CARING ABOUT WHAT PEOPLE THINK

This one is a HUGE dream killer, how many of us do not express ourselves honestly for fear of what others will think? How many of us are putting on a mask which hides our deepest desires, our real thoughts and ideas, and who we truly are on a soul level? I would say the vast majority of the Planet have this mental schism, I used to have it myself.

I love the David Icke quote 'The greatest prison people live in is the fear of what others think about them' and never has a truer sentence been spoken. Many of us will go through our lives trying to impress people that not only do we not care about, but oftentimes they don't really care about us either!

We are all trying to fit into this sheep pen not realising that there are acres of open fields that lay beyond! We police each other, the so-called 'powers that be' don't even have to do that anymore because anyone who thinks outside of the box is called a weirdo, nerd, or conspiracy theorist and therefore outcasted from the rest of the sheep.

There is something within the human psyche that needs to feel accepted by everyone else, the need not to be excluded in a sense. I guess its natural to want to be liked, although for myself I really couldn't care less these days. I think that 6 years of speaking unpopular truths and several smear campaigns have beaten that out of me! On the flip side, what that has given me is absolute total freedom to express who I really am, that has enabled me to feel as though I am living my true purpose now because its no holds barred.

The ironic thing about caring about what people think that makes it such a complete waste of time is that you can never in a million years control their opinion! Ok you can put up a facade of being a certain person that may get you some friends, but then you aren't being authentic, you're essentially living a lie. Most people are so full of emotional baggage, unhealed traumas, stress, and other issues that even if there is nothing not to like in your character then they will find something! That's because most people project their pain onto others.

> **BAD NEWS IS:**
>
> You cannot make people like,
> love, understand, validate, accept
> or be nice to you.
> You can't control them either.
>
> **GOOD NEWS IS:**
>
> It doesn't matter.

In the early days in my own life I couldn't tell you the amount of time and energy wasted on trying to please and be accepted by others, even at school I was desperate to get in with the 'in crowd' which never really worked either!

I have to say again the emotional work I have done on myself has helped tremendously. Wanting to be liked by everyone is a self-love and self-worth issue, or lack thereof. If you don't really value yourself then you're going to be looking constantly for others to validate you. This is what we see so much on social media, many people who have very little self-love attempting to get it through dopamine hits on Facebook likes.

Self-love isn't an overnight thing for most of us, it takes hard work and a lot of healing to get there, even if we have had relatively good childhoods. But again this quick fix society is constantly looking for shortcuts to the inconvenient work of doing the self-healing which will essentially bring them what they want if they are committed and determined enough to walk that path through to the end.

I see this in my own sessions I run, there are two types of people. One group who are 100% committed and see the process out until the end which can take many months, and then of course, reap the rewards, and others that give it lip service then give up after a few weeks. They then wonder why they still have issues in their life that won't go away. The equation is simple self love=not caring what others think=freedom to live an authentic life=in line with purpose.

I always wonder this, why would you want to be liked by most people anyway? I mean look at what folk believe in? They put more importance on getting drunk, eating junk food, and sporting events. The level of consciousness on this Planet is so low right now that nobody should be aspiring to follow the herd, because the herd is essentially heading over a cliff face!

Even something like fashion boggles, the mind, why on Earth would you want to look like everyone else? It makes no sense, we are supposed to be individuals who are expressing their individuality not trying to copy each other. I think it looks horrendous that other people try and copy how each other look!

No, I say be authentically you, and walk out of the prison cell you have put yourself in.

LAUGH AT THE INSANITY

Sometimes you just have to take a step back and laugh at the insanity of it all, there is certainly a very serious side to it all which cannot be ignored but having the fundamental understanding that you're living in what is essentially a mental asylum can actually help you see through the cosmic joke.

Just the fact that humans believe themselves to be powerless when in fact we are powerful beyond measure is laughable in itself. How a tiny number of people have kept billions of people locked down in consciousness is also unreal when you stop to dwell on it.

Without doubt, there is much work for us to do if we are going to evolve out of this mess, and having a sense of humor amid the craziness really can put things into perspective. How people think voting for a psychopathic puppet represents freedom is very amusing, how others have taken Religious doctrines so literally beggars belief, and don't even get me started on people chasing Pokemon around parks, or tipping buckets of ice over their head!

Now we have over 40 kinds of genders. You can literally wake up in the morning and now decide you want to be either a man, a woman, or neither! I have seen accounts of people identifying with animals and even babies!

I read one article the other day where now it is possible to marry yourself, and people are! Trying to look at it all from a higher perspective in that it is one big computer game that we need to work our way through helps deal with the magnitude of it all. Don't forget to laugh at it all sometimes it helps to cope with the enormity of the tasks that lie ahead. We will get through this and we will transcend our current level of consciousness to become the creative, artistic, and loving geniuses once again when we snap out of thsi amnesia!

I hope you enjoyed this ebook, for session enquires please email me tony@transcendingtimes.org For details and purchase of my other books click here https://transcendingtimes.org/books/ Please also consider subscribing to my weekly newsletter at https://transcendingtimes.org/subscribe-to-newsletters/

Made in United States
North Haven, CT
11 March 2022

16982461R00036